AF540097

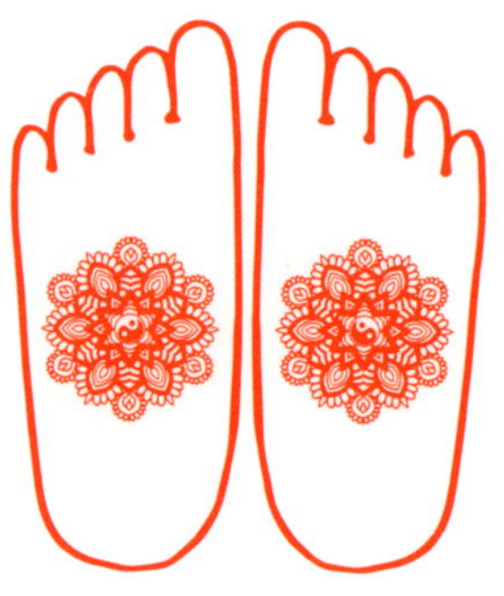

"Racism is a heart disease. How we think and respond is at the core of racial suffering and racial healing. If we cannot think clearly and respond wisely, we will continue to damage the world's heart."

RUTH KING

An international meditation teacher at the Insight Meditation Tradition, known for her work on mindfulness and emotional healing.

"If you meditate in perfect peace and then flash someone an irritable look because they make noise or their child cries, you are entirely missing the point."

KHANDRO RINPOCHE

Tibetan lama and teacher, known for her teachings on Tibetan Buddhism and women's roles.

The
Buddha
Way
Mind
Over
Matter

Published 2025

FiNGERPRINT!

Prakash Books

Fingerprint Publishing
@FingerprintP
@fingerprintpublishingbooks
www.fingerprintpublishing.com

ISBN: 978 93 7089 924 7

Contents

Curious About Buddhism?

Let's Dive In!

- Buddhism was founded by Siddhartha Gautama, also known as the Buddha, in the 5th century BCE in modern-day Nepal and Northeast India.

- Siddhartha Gautama was born into a royal family, but he renounced his privileged life in search of liberation from the suffering he saw all around him.

- After years of ascetic practice and meditation, he attained enlightenment under the Bodhi tree in Bodh Gaya, India. This earned him the title "Buddha," which means "the Enlightened One."

- The Buddha spent the rest of his life teaching dharma or the truths he had discovered.

- His teachings were initially passed down orally by his disciples and later written down in various texts.

- The first Sangha or Buddhist community consisted of monks and nuns who followed the Buddha's teachings and lived a monastic life dedicated to spiritual practice.

Famous Faces on the Buddhist Path

The following personalities
inspire and guide individuals
in the pursuit of a virtuous
and tranquil life continually.

Their quotes encapsulate
the essence of Buddhist philosophy,
emphasizing self-control, rationality
and alignment with nature.

"The present moment is the only time over which we have dominion."

THICH NHAT HANH

Vietnamese Zen monk and peace activist, renowned for his work on mindfulness and the Engaged Buddhism movement.

"You are the sky. Everything else – it's just the weather."

PEMA CHÖDRÖN

America-born Tibetan Buddhist nun and author, known for her teachings on compassion and overcoming fear.

*"The heart is like a garden.
It can grow compassion or fear,
resentment or love. What seeds
will you plant there?"*

JACK KORNFIELD

American Buddhist teacher and author, a prominent figure in the mindfulness movement.

"We need the compassion and the courage to change the conditions that support our suffering. Those conditions are things like ignorance, bitterness, negligence, clinging, and holding on."

SHARON SALZBERG

American meditation teacher and author, co-founder of the Insight Meditation Society.

"The answer lies within ourselves. If we can't find peace and happiness there, it's not going to come from the outside."

TENZIN PALMO

British Tibetan Buddhist nun and teacher known for her commitment to women's role in Tibetan Buddhism.

Discover the Main Paths

Let's Learn About the Major Schools

Theravada
Buddhism

Meaning the "teachings of the elders," Theravada Buddhism is the oldest form of Buddhism and is prevalent in Sri Lanka, Thailand, Myanmar, Laos and Cambodia.

It is based on the Pali Canon of scriptures and emphasizes individual enlightenment through meditation and adherence to the monastic code.

Mahayana
Buddhism

Meaning "great vehicle," Mahayana Buddhism developed around the 1st century BCE and spread to China, Korea, Japan, Vietnam and other parts of East Asia.

It introduces the concept of the Bodhisattva, a being who seeks enlightenment not only for themself but for all sentient beings.

Major Mahayana texts include the *Prajnaparamita Sutras* and the *Lotus Sutra*.

Vajrayana
Buddhism

Meaning "the way of the diamond," Vajrayana or Tibetan Buddhism developed in Tibet and the Himalayan region around the 7th century CE.

It incorporates complex rituals, visualization and esoteric practices aimed at achieving rapid enlightenment.

Famous Faces on the Buddhist Path

"People think meditating is sitting there, nobody bothering you, but you can even talk and still meditate."

JET LI

Chinese martial artist and actor, follower of Tibetan Buddhism.

"Our thoughts, like the ocean waves, are always in motion. Let them be."

TARTHANG TULKU RINPOCHE

Tibetan lama from the Nyingma tradition, is the founder of the Nyingma Institute in Berkeley, California and is known for his work on healing, time and human potential.

"Self-reflection is a practice, a path, and an attitude. It is the spirit of taking an interest in that which we usually try to push away."

DZIGAR KONGTRUL RINPOCHE

Tibetan lama from the Nyingma tradition, teacher of philosophy and meditation, has authored books on Buddhist wisdom.

"Together on the path of love, we can try to make a small difference in someone's life. What else is there to do?"

CHAN KHONG

Vietnamese Buddhist nun and peace activist, closely associated with Thich Nhat Hanh and the Plum Village tradition.

"Anything which is troubling you, anything which is irritating you, THAT is your teacher."

AJAHN CHAH

Thai Forest Tradition monk known for his teachings on mindfulness and simplicity.

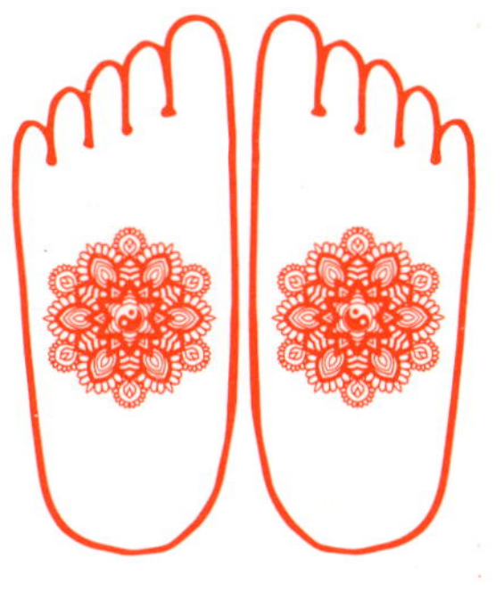

Buddhism 101

Core Teachings

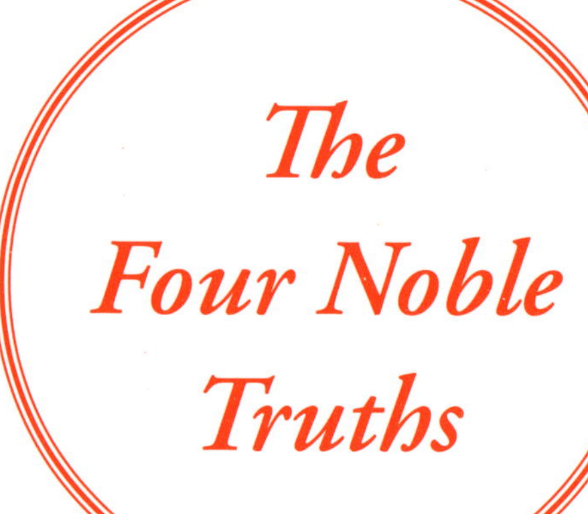
The
Four Noble
Truths

Suffering (Dukkha)

Life involves suffering and dissatisfaction which manifests in various forms, from obvious physical pain to subtle mental distress.

Origin of Suffering (Samudaya)

Suffering arises from desire, attachment and unawareness about the true nature of reality.

Cessation of Suffering (Nirodha)

Suffering can end by eliminating desire and attachment.

Path to the Cessation of Suffering (Magga)

The path to end suffering is the Noble Eightfold Path.

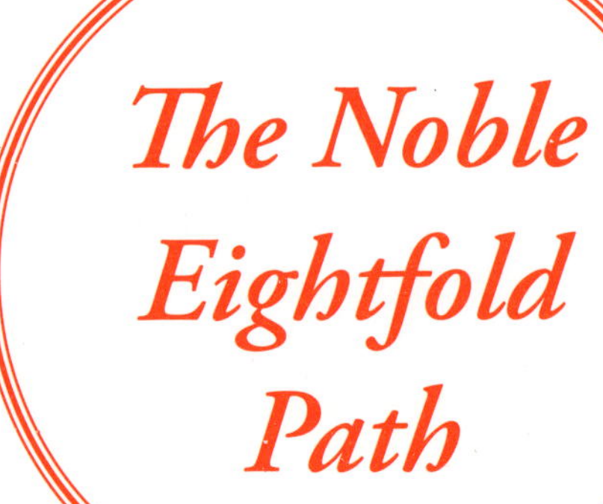
The Noble
Eightfold
Path

Right View

Understanding the Four Noble Truths and the nature of reality.

Right Resolve

Committing to freeing oneself of suffering.

Right Speech

Speaking truthfully and kindly.

Right Action

Acting ethically, avoiding harm to others.

Right Livelihood

Earning a living in a way that does not harm others.

Right Effort

Cultivating a positive state of mind and avoiding negative thought processes.

Right Mindfulness

Developing awareness of the body, feelings, mind and phenomena.

Right Concentration

Developing mental focus through meditation.

The Three
Marks of
Existence

Impermanence (Anicca)

Everything in life is transient and constantly changing.

Suffering (Dukkha)

Life is full of suffering and dissatisfaction.

No Self (Anatta)

There is no unchanging, eternal self or soul.

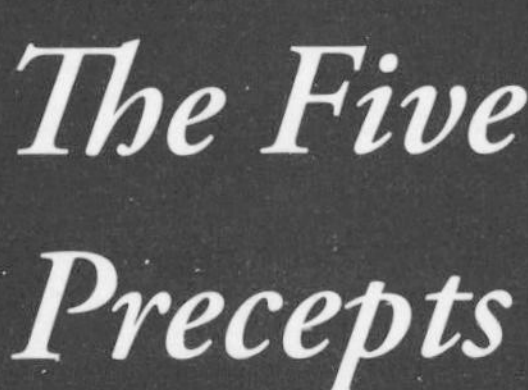

The Five Precepts

Abstain from taking life.

Non-violence and respect for all living beings.

Abstain from taking what is not given.

Honesty and respect for others' property.

Abstain from sexual misconduct.

Maintaining integrity in relationships by not indulging in adultery.

Abstain from false speech.

Being truthful and avoiding harmful speech.

Abstain from intoxicants that cloud the mind.

Clarity and mindfulness in daily life.

Famous Faces on the Buddhist Path

"It may not be entirely pleasant at first to embrace your fear, pain or grief, but with mindfulness you can hold them as a mother holds her crying baby, and you can feel safe even when the storm of strong emotions moves through you and out into the air and the Earth."

NGUYEN ANH HONG

Vietnamese Zen master known for his teachings on mindfulness and meditation.

"There is the in-breath and there is the out-breath, and too often we feel like we have to exhale all the time. The inhale is absolutely essential-and then you can exhale."

ROSHI JOAN HALIFAX

American Zen Buddhist teacher and author, known for her work in end-of-life care.

"You should never be ashamed of the suffering you've been through."

ROBERT THURMAN

American Buddhist scholar and author, a prominent advocate of Tibetan Buddhism in the West.

"We need to train our mind because it is the mind which makes us suffer."

RINGU TULKU RINPOCHE

Tibetan Lama and scholar, known for his teachings on Tibetan Buddhism and meditation.

"How we interpret information and our experiences of the world depends entirely on how much merit we have accumulated."

DZONGSAR KHYENTSE RINPOCHE

Tibetan Buddhist teacher and filmmaker, known for his teachings and films on Buddhism.

The Handbook of a Buddhist

Key Values to Hold On To

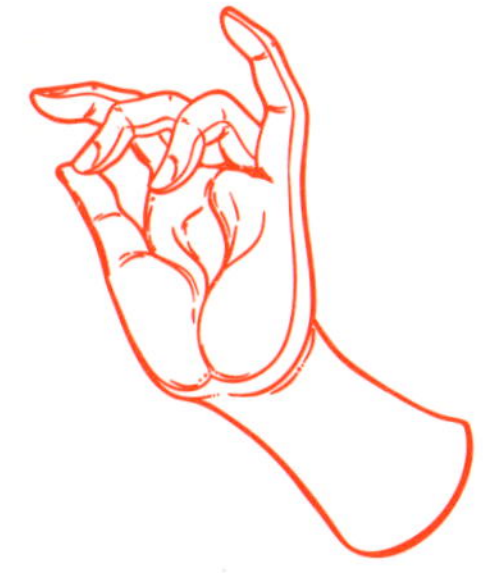

IMPERMANENCE (ANICCA)

Everything in life is transient and constantly changing. Acknowledging impermanence helps in reducing attachment and suffering.

NON-SELF (ANATTA)

The self or soul is an ever-evolving, fleeting being. Understanding this concept helps in diminishing ego and selfish desires.

KARMA

Actions have consequences: good actions lead to positive outcomes, while harmful actions lead to negative outcomes. This principle encourages ethical behavior and personal responsibility.

COMPASSION (KARUNA)

Developing compassion for all living beings is central to Buddhism. This principle promotes kindness, empathy and a desire to alleviate the suffering of others.

MINDFULNESS (SATI)

It involves being fully present and aware of the current moment. Practicing mindfulness helps cultivate inner peace, clarity and understanding.

MEDITATION (BHAVANA)

Develops concentration, insight and mental discipline. Various forms of meditation are employed to cultivate mindfulness and wisdom.

ETHICAL CONDUCT (SILA)

Forming the foundation for a harmonious and peaceful life, it involves adhering to moral precepts, such as not harming others, being truthful and living with integrity.

WISDOM (PANNA)

Points to the deep understanding of the true nature of reality, which includes the impermanence of all things, the inevitability of suffering and the absence of a permanent self. Cultivating such wisdom leads to enlightenment and liberation from the cycle of birth and death.

DEPENDENT ORIGINATION (PRATITYASAMUTPADA)

Everything occurs as a reaction to multiple conditions. This principle explains the interconnectedness of all phenomena and the cause-and-effect nature of existence.

MIDDLE WAY (MADHYAMAKA)

It is a balanced approach to spiritual practice that leads to enlightenment by avoiding extremes of self-indulgence and self-mortification.

LOVING-KINDNESS (METTA)

This practice involves developing unconditional love, a heart full of kindness and goodwill toward all beings.

EQUANIMITY (UPEKKHA)

It is the practice of being impartial and balanced in all circumstances by maintaining mental calmness and evenness of temper.

GENEROSITY (DANA)

This practice, of giving and sharing without expecting anything in return, cultivates a sense of selflessness and compassion.

PATIENCE (KHANTI)

It is the ability to endure hardships without feeling agitated or losing one's temper. It is a crucial quality for developing a calm and composed mind.

ENERGY (VIRIYA)

The persistent application of effort in one's spiritual practice, it involves enthusiasm and perseverance in following the path to enlightenment.

TRUTHFULNESS (SACCA)

It extends beyond mere speech to include living in alignment with the truth. It involves honesty, integrity and being transparent to oneself and others.

RENUNCIATION (NEKKHAMMA)

The voluntary giving up of worldly pleasures and attachments, it is not deprivation but freeing oneself from the bonds of material desires to focus on spiritual growth.

By embracing these additional principles, practitioners of Buddhism can enhance their spiritual development, leading to a profound understanding of the path to enlightenment.

Famous Faces on the Buddhist Path

"To be free of the discriminating is to manifest miraculous awareness-awareness that is miraculously simple, miraculously unadorned."

GEOFFREY SHUGEN ARNOLD

American Zen priest and author, known for his teachings on Zen Buddhism.

"If our hearts are ready for anything, we are touched by the beauty and poetry and mystery that fill our world."

TARA BRACH

American psychologist and meditation teacher, known for her work on mindfulness and self-compassion.

“To embrace suffering culminates in greater empathy, the capacity to feel what it is like for the other to suffer, which is the ground for unsentimental compassion and love.”

STEPHEN BATCHELOR

Scottish author and teacher of secular Buddhism, known for his leadership roles in meditation retreats.

Buddhism and the World

How Buddhist Teachings Impact Worldly Matters

Buddhism, with its rich history and profound teachings, offers a steady path to spiritual awakening and freedom from suffering.

By understanding its origins, historical development and core principles, one can appreciate the depth and relevance of this ancient tradition in contemporary life.

Despite the distinctions in the Theravada, Mahayana or Vajrayana schools, the essence of Buddhism remains to be about the pursuit of wisdom, ethical conduct and mental discipline that leads to enlightenment.

BUDDHISM AND ENVIRONMENTAL ETHICS

Buddhism's emphasis on interconnectedness and respect for all living beings provide a robust framework for environmental ethics. Exploring how Buddhist principles guide sustainable living and ecological conservation offers a fresh perspective on contemporary environmental challenges.

BUDDHISM AND SOCIAL JUSTICE

Buddhism's teachings on compassion (karuna) and loving-kindness (metta) have significant implications for social justice. Investigating how these principles inform and inspire movements for equality, human rights and social change can be deeply enlightening.

BUDDHISM AND MODERN PSYCHOLOGY

There is a seamless integration of Buddhist mindfulness and meditation practices into modern psychological methods, such as Mindfulness-Based Stress Reduction and Mindfulness-Based Cognitive Therapy. Further, exploring the synergy between such Buddhist praxis and modern psychology can enhance mental health treatments.

BUDDHISM AND TECHNOLOGY

In an age of digital distraction, Buddhist teachings on mindfulness and staying grounded in the present offer valuable insights into managing technology use. Exploring how Buddhist principles can help maintain digital well-being and prevent addiction to technology is a vital area of study.

BUDDHISM AND EDUCATION

Integrating Buddhist mindfulness practices into educational settings foster emotional intelligence, concentration and ethical development in students. Investigating the benefits and methods of incorporating these practices in schools and universities can revolutionize education.

BUDDHISM AND PHYSICAL HEALTH

Buddhist principles of moderation, mindfulness and ethical living significantly impact physical health. Exploring how these teachings guide healthy lifestyle choices, stress management and holistic well-being can be profoundly beneficial.

BUDDHISM AND CREATIVITY

Buddhist meditational practices enhance creative processes in art, literature and other creative fields. Investigating the relationship between Buddhism and creativity can reveal new ways to unlock artistic potential.

BUDDHISM AND BUSINESS ETHICS

Applying Buddhist principles to business ethics promote integrity, compassion and social responsibility in the corporate world. Exploring how these teachings can guide ethical decision-making and corporate governance is crucial.

BUDDHISM AND INTERPERSONAL RELATIONSHIPS

Buddhist teachings on loving-kindness, compassion and non-attachment deeply influence how we relate to others. Investigating how these principles can enhance interpersonal relationships and resolve conflicts is highly valuable.

BUDDHISM AND POLITICAL THEORY

Buddhist principles inform ethical leadership, governance and policymaking. Exploring how these teachings can guide political decision-making and promote peace and justice in society is a promising area of study.

By delving deeper into these aspects, we can uncover the profound relevance and applicability of Buddhist principles to various facets of modern life, enriching our understanding and practice of the philosophy of Buddhism.

Famous Faces on the Buddhist Path

"When we accept what is in this very moment, without pushing or pulling, when there is no running after or running away, we find in our practice a level of deep acceptance and peace."

MICHAEL STONE

Canadian Buddhist teacher and author, known for his teachings on mindfulness and social justice.

"In this world everything changes except good deeds and bad deeds; these follow you as the shadow follows the body."

VENERABLE BHIKKHU BODHI

American Theravada Buddhist monk, known for his translations of Pali texts and teachings.

"Be kind to yourself as you proceed along this journey. This kindness, in itself, is a means of awakening the spark of love within you and helping others to discover that spark within themselves."

TSOKNYI RINPOCHE

Tibetan Lama and teacher, known for his teachings on Dzogchen and meditation.

"If we could not be bought by praise or defeated by criticism, we would have incredible strength."

DZONGSAR KHYENTSE RINPOCHE

Tibetan Buddhist teacher and filmmaker, known for his teachings and films on Buddhism.

"The crucial thing is to be mindful of what is occurring, not to control what is occurring."

BHANTE HENEPOLA GUNARATANA

Sri Lankan Theravada monk, author of *Mindfulness in Plain English* and a key figure in spreading mindfulness meditation worldwide.

"One cannot always have joyful occasions, joyful thoughts in one's own life, but if one has joy with other people, one can surely find something to be happy about."

AYYA KHEMA

German-born Buddhist nun and teacher, known for her work on women's roles in Buddhism.

"The reason we are unhappy is because we have extreme craving for sense objects—samsaric objects—and we grasp at them. We are seeking to solve our problems, but we are not seeking in the right place. The right place is our ego-grasping."

LAMA THUBTEN YESHE

Tibetan Lama and founder of the FPMT, known for his teachings on Tibetan Buddhism.

"To become aware of your own limits is to become aware of your own fear. You don't have to reject your fear or transcend it. All you need to do is recognize your fear and be a witness to it."

ANAM THUBTEN

Tibetan Lama, founder of the Dharmata Foundation, known for his teachings on the nature of mind and meditation.

"I suggest that if you were able to focus your attention at will, you could actually choose the universe you appear to inhabit."

BRUCE ALAN WALLACE

American author and expert on Tibetan Buddism, founder of the Santa Barbara Institute for Consciousness Studies.

"What is the world full of? It is full of things that arise, persist, and cease. Grasp and cling to them, and they produce suffering. Don't grasp and cling to them, and they do not produce suffering."

ACHARYA BUDDHADASA

Thai Buddhist teacher and scholar, known for his innovative teachings on the Dharma and social engagement.

"If there is no peace in the minds of individuals, how can there be peace in the world? Make peace in your own mind first."

S.N. GOENKA

Indian teacher and founder of Vipassana Meditation centers, known for his work on meditation, was awarded Padma Bhushan by the Government of India.

"All that we are looking for in life—all the happiness, contentment, and peace of mind—is right here in the present moment."

YONGEY MINGYUR RINPOCHE

Tibetan Buddhist teacher, known for his teachings that offer a blend of traditional Buddhist practices to modern science.

"By nurturing the shadow elements of our being with infinite generosity, we can access the state of luminous awareness and undermine ego."

LAMA TSULTRIM ALLIONE

American Tibetan Buddhist teacher, known for her work on women's empowerment and the Five Dakini Practice.

"Happiness is a state of inner fulfillment, not the gratification of inexhaustible desires for outward things."

MATTHIEU RICARD

Nepalese French Buddhist monk and author, known for his work on happiness and altruism.

"Silence is so much more productive of wisdom and clarity than thinking."

AJAHN BRAHM

Trained in the Thai Forest Tradition of Theravada Buddhism, he is a British-born monk, known for his teachings on mindfulness and meditation.

"Concentration grows through the willingness to encounter, understand, and eventually remove all that agitates the mind."

SHAILA CATHERINE

American meditation teacher and author, known for her work on Vipassana meditation.

"Realization is not knowledge about the universe, but the living experience of the nature of the universe. Until we have such living experience, we remain dependent on examples, and subject to their limits."

CHÖGYAL NAMKHAI NORBU

Tibetan Lama and author, known for his teachings on Dzogchen and meditation.

"Confidence is the willingness to be as ridiculous, luminous, intelligent, and kind as you really are, without embarrassment."

SUSAN PIVER

American author and meditation teacher, known for her work on mindfulness and relationships.

"Letting go is wholesome and healing . . . As soon as we let go of the things we hanker after and set them free, without holding on to anything, we experience freedom and joy that are unmediated and real."

CHÖKYI NYIMA RINPOCHE

Tibetan Buddhist teacher and meditation master, known for his teachings on Mahamudra and Dzogchen.

"In considering the substantial self, it is important to make a clear distinction between the self itself and the mere attribution of self."

KHENCHEN THRANGU RINPOCHE

Karma Kagyu scholar and teacher, known for his work on Tibetan Buddhism and meditation.

"Abiding in the space of the nature of mind, we not only are free, we are freedom."

TENZIN WANGYAL RINPOCHE

Tibetan Lama and author, known for his teachings on Bon Tibetan tradition and meditation.

"Let me give you a wonderful Zen practice. Wake up in the morning . . . look in the mirror, and laugh at yourself."

ROSHI BERNIE GLASSMAN

American Zen teacher and founder of the Zen Peacemakers, known for his work on social activism and Zen practice.

"Beings are the owners of their actions, the heirs of their actions; they spring from their actions, are bound to their actions, and are supported by their actions. Whatever deeds they do, good or bad, of those they shall be heirs."

VENERABLE BHIKKHU BODHI

American Theravada Buddhist monk, known for his translations of Pali texts and teachings.

"Open your heart, open your eyes, caring, acting, serving. Thus we live our lives; crossing, crossing over from suffering to compassion."

ROSHI PAT ENKYO O'HARA

Soto Zen priest and teacher in the Zen Buddhist tradition, known for her work on Zen practice and social justice.

"Mainly it is important to remember the kindness of the Buddha and abide in that remembrance."

H.E. CHODEN RINPOCHE

Tibetan Lama and teacher, known for his teachings on Mahayana Buddhism.

"Without inner peace, outer peace is impossible. We all wish for world peace, but world peace will never be achieved unless we first establish peace within our own minds."

VENERABLE GESHE KELSANG GYATSO

Tibetan Buddhist monk and teacher, known for his work on modern Buddhism and meditation.

"Some of us are drawn to mountains the way the moon draws the tide. Both the great forests and the mountains live in my bones. They have taught me, humbled me, purified me and changed me."

ROSHI JOAN HALIFAX

American Zen teacher and author, known for her work in end-of-life care and mindfulness.

"We believe that with the wisdom, compassion and the good concentration that comes from the practise of Buddhism, we will eventually be able to penetrate through illusion and relieve our suffering, and the suffering of those around us."

VENERABLE THICH PHUOC TAN

Vietnamese Buddhist monk, known for his teachings on meditation and mindfulness.

". . . as unlikely as it may sound, in fact this sorrow is the gateway to lasting happiness, the kind that can never be taken from you."

SUSAN PIVER

American author and meditation teacher, known for her work on mindfulness and relationships.

"Be kind to yourself as you proceed along this journey. This kindness, in itself, is a means of awakening the spark of love within you and helping others to discover that spark within themselves."

TSOKNYI RINPOCHE

Tibetan Lama and teacher, known for his teachings on Dzogchen and meditation.

"When we recognize that the seemingly object nature of reality is nothing different than the subject nature of mind, which is rigpa, it is called enlightenment."

DZOGCHEN PONLOP RINPOCHE

Abbot of Dzogchen Monastery, known for his teachings on Dzogchen and meditation.

"I swore to fight fanaticism and mercilessness, and to devote my entire life to pursuing justice through Buddhism's teachings on non-violence, tolerance, and mercy."

VENERABLE THICH QUANG DO

Vietnamese Mahayana Buddhist monk, known for his teachings on Zen practice and social activism.

"We cannot understand many of our problems because our way of thinking is generally based on ignorance which is the cause of imagination or illusion. (You and Your Problems)"

VENERABLE K. SRI DHAMMANANDA

Sri Lankan Buddhist monk, known for his teachings on Theravada Buddhism.

"Any place you don't want to be, no matter how comfortable, is a prison for you."

AJAHN BRAHM

Trained in the Thai Forest Tradition of Theravada Buddhism, he is a British-born monk, known for his teachings on mindfulness and meditation.

"... there is no 'I' beyond our basic consciousness, no 'I' different from the experience. The experience is everything. We do not have any ownership over it."

RINGU TULKU RINPOCHE

Tibetan Buddhist Master belonging to the Kangyu order, known for his teachings on Tibetan Buddhism and meditation.

"Cherishing others opens the door to every happiness for self and others."

THUBTEN ZOPA RINPOCHE

Nepalese Lama and spiritual director of the FPMT, known for his teachings on Tibetan Buddhism.

"If one achieves the true virtues of peace and joy, then the path of wisdom and compassion will naturally open up, and one will know what needs to be done."

VENERABLE THICH PHUOC TINH

Vietnamese Zen master, known for his teachings on mindfulness and meditation.

"We don't wish for suffering, but once we understand how to be in relationship with it, it becomes the means through which we mature as loving and wise people."

ṬHĀNISSARO BHIKKHU

American Buddhist monk and author, abbot of the Metta Forest Monastery in California.

*"When we don't ask,
we don't let others give.
When we fear rejection,
we don't let generosity arise."*

ROSHI BERNIE GLASSMAN

American Zen teacher and founder of the Zen Peacemakers, known for his work on social activism and Zen practice.

"Love is the real nuclear bomb that destroys all our enemies, because when we love all living beings, we have no enemies."

VENERABLE GESHE KELSANG GYATSO

Tibetan Buddhist monk and teacher, known for his work on modern Buddhism and meditation.

"I get it now; I didn't get it then. That life is about losing and about doing it as gracefully as possible . . . and enjoying everything in between."

MIA FARROW

American actress and activist, follower of Tibetan Buddhism.

"What we all have in common is an appreciation of kindness and compassion; all the religions have this. We all lean towards love."

RICHARD GERE

American actor and humanitarian, a long-time supporter of the Dalai Lama and Tibetan causes.

"Sometimes, you've got to let everything go—purge yourself. If you are unhappy with anything . . . whatever is bringing you down, get rid of it. Because you'll find that when you're free, your true creativity, your true self comes out."

TINA TURNER

American singer and actress, practiced Nichiren Buddhism and credited it with helping her overcome personal struggles.

"We have to make good use of the time we have. That simple. We have to wake up every day, knowing that it's not just an ordinary day. We have to take the moment, seize each day."

ORLANDO BLOOM

British actor, known for his practice of Nichiren Buddhism and belief in the power of chanting.

"I have witnessed the softening of the hardest of hearts by a simple smile."

GOLDIE HAWN

American actress and producer, practices mindfulness and meditation influenced by Buddhist principles.

"If you have been brutally broken, but still have the courage to be gentle to other living beings, then you're a badass with the heart of an angel."

KEANU REEVES

Canadian actor, known for his interest in Buddhism and Eastern philosophy.

"Remembering that you are going to die is the best way I know to avoid the trap of thinking you have something to lose. You are already naked. There is no reason not to follow your heart."

STEVE JOBS

Co-founder of Apple Inc., practiced Zen Buddhism and was influenced by its principles in his personal and professional life.

“There is a crack in everything,
that’s how the light gets in.”

LEONARD COHEN

Canadian singer-songwriter and poet, ordained as a Rinkai Zen Buddhist monk, who took the name “Jikan.”

"It is people's hearts that move the age."

HERBIE HANCOCK

American jazz musician and composer, practices Nichiren Buddhism and attributes his creative success to it.

"I like when life is sort of spontaneous. I like the unexpected. I'm comfortable in that!"

KATE HUDSON

American actress, practices mindfulness and meditation influenced by Buddhist teachings.

"Never underestimate the power of jealousy and the power of envy to destroy. Never underestimate that."

OLIVER STONE

American filmmaker and screenwriter, follows Buddhist philosophy and has been influenced by its principles in his work.

"You've got to take care of yourself on the path, not just when you cross the goal line, because don't forget, wherever you are, that's the goal line."

JEFF BRIDGES

American actor, practices Zen Buddhism and integrates its teachings into his life and work.

"You have to make peace with yourself. The key is to find the harmony in what you have."

NAOMI WATTS

British actress, practices meditation and follows Buddhist principles for peace and balance.

"Awakening does not mean a change in difficulty, it means a change in how those difficulties are met."

MARK EPSTEIN

American author and psychotherapist, who found a synthesis between Shakyamuni and Freud.

"Developing our sympathetic compassion is not only possible but the only reason for us to be here on earth."

GEORGE SAUNDERS

American author, practices meditation and follows Buddhist principles in his writing and life.

"Go find something that you haven't done before. Don't do the same thing over and over again."

MIKE SHINODA

American musician, co-founder of Linkin Park, practices meditation and follows Buddhist principles.

"Your art kind of changes as you get older, by nature of the fact that you're hopefully gaining wisdom and you're starting to watch things with a better overview."

SHERYL CROW

American singer-songwriter, follows Buddhist practices like meditation for personal growth.

"The reason that everybody likes planning is that nobody has to do anything."

JERRY BROWN

Former Governor of California, practices Zen Buddhism and incorporates its principles into his political and personal life.